GIBSIDE

Gateshead

THE NATIONAL TRUST

Acknowledgements

The tour chapter of this guide has been written by Dr Margaret Wills; for this and all her work on Gibside the National Trust is most grateful. The rest is by Oliver Garnett, who would also like to thank Harry Beamish, Hugh Dixon, Jane Munro and Pamela Wallhead for their help. The following sources have been particularly useful: Ralph Arnold, *The Unhappy Countess*, London, 1957; Jesse Foot, *The Lives of Andrew Robinson Bowes, Esq, and the Countess of Strathmore*, London, n.d. [1810]; William Fordyce, *The History and Antiquities of the County Palatine of Durham*, Newcastle, 1855, ii, p.694; J. Gill, *Streatlam and Gibside*, Durham, 1980; Charles E. Hardy, *John Bowes and the Bowes Museum*, Bishop Auckland, 1970; Margaret Hudson, 'Pillar of Patriotism', *Country Life*, 27 December 1979, pp.2460–1; Edward Hughes, *North Country Life in the Eighteenth Century: The North East, 1700–1750*, Oxford, 1952; Christopher Hussey, 'Gibside, I, II', *Country Life*, cxi, 8, 15 February 1952, pp.354–7, 422–5; William Hutchinson, *The History and Antiquities of the County Palatine of Durham*, Newcastle, 1787, ii, pp.451–2; Mary Eleanor Bowes, Countess of Strathmore, *The Confessions of the Countess of Strathmore written by herself*, London, 1793; Robert Surtees, *History and Antiquities of the County Palatine of Durham*, London, 1820, ii, pp.252–70; Margaret Wills, *Gibside and the Bowes Family*, Newcastle, 1995.

The Banqueting House is owned by the Landmark Trust, an independent preservation charity that rescues architecturally interesting buildings and lets them for self-catering holidays. Full details are available in the Landmark Trust Handbook, price £9.50, including post and packing, refundable against the first booking. For copies, telephone 01628 825 925, or write to Shottesbrooke, Maidenhead, Berkshire SL6 3SW.

Photographs: Bowes Museum, Barnard Castle, Co. Durham pp.4, 5 (top), 26, 30, 31; British Architectural Library, RIBA, London pp.17, 18; Syndics of the Fitzwilliam Museum, Cambridge p.27 (bottom right); Landmark Trust p.7; Metropolitan Museum of Art, New York p.23; National Gallery of Scotland p.1; National Portrait Gallery, London p.5 (bottom right), 28; National Trust pp.13, 14 (bottom), 20; NT/Colin Dixon pp.10, 14 (top); NT/Will Walker p.32; National Trust Photographic Library/Nick Meers front cover, pp.9, 11, 55, 16, 19, 21, 24–5, back cover; The Royal Collection © 2005 Her Majesty Queen Elizabeth II p.29; Earl of Strathmore and Kinghorne/Durham County Record Office p.8; Strathmore Estates, Glamis Castle/Pilgrim Press pp.5 (bottom left), 22, 27 (top left).

First published in Great Britain in 1999 by the National Trust

© 1999 The National Trust

Registered charity no. 205846

ISBN 1 84359 207 X

Revised 2005

Designed by James Shurmur

Phototypeset in Monotype Bembo Series 270
by Intraspan Ltd, Smallfield, Surrey

Print managed by Astron
for National Trust Enterprises Ltd, Heelis, Kemble Drive, Swindon SN2 2NA

(*Front cover*) The Chapel from the Long Walk

(*Title-page*) *A View of Gibside from Goodshield Haugh in the late eighteenth century*; by Edward Dayes (National Gallery of Scotland)

(*Back cover*) The Long Walk from the portico of the Chapel, with the Column to Liberty on the horizon

CONTENTS

GIBSIDE

All the gentlemen are planting and adorning their Seats, but nothing comes up to the grandeur and magnificence of what Mr Bowes has done and is a doing.

Edward Montagu, 1753

Gibside was essentially the work of one man – the fiery-tempered, music-loving coal baron GEORGE BOWES. Between 1729 and 1760 he transformed the wooded eastern slopes of the Derwent Valley to make a landscape garden on a heroic scale. His creation was a subtle mixture of old and new ideas, combining straight, formal vistas, such as the Long Walk, with the more irregular planting and me-andering paths and streams that epitomise the eight-eenth-century English landscape garden. Key points in the design were marked by garden build-ings, designed in a range of styles by two of the North-East's leading architects, Daniel Garrett and James Paine: a Palladian bath house and stables, a Gothick banqueting house and a Column to Liberty, celebrating Bowes's loyalty to the political ideals of the Whig party. Almost the only building which was not incorporated into the grand design was the old Jacobean mansion, which Bowes left unmodernised, perhaps for lack of money. He was determined, however, to be buried in style, and while he lay dying in 1760, he began building the

Gibside from the south, c.1817; by J. M. W. Turner (Bowes Museum)

Gibside from the north, c.1817; by J. M. W. Turner (Bowes Museum)

Palladian Chapel at the southern end of the Long Walk as his mausoleum.

This princely inheritance passed to Bowes's only child, Mary Eleanor, who from an early age had been fascinated by gardening and built the Orangery in 1772–4. Alas, Gibside brought her nothing but grief. She was married unhappily to the 9th Earl of Strathmore, and then even more disastrously to an unscrupulous fortune-hunter, Andrew Robinson Stoney, who was eventually imprisoned after kidnapping her at gunpoint. Stoney treated Gibside and its tenants no better, cutting down much of the mature woodland to pay his gambling debts.

Mary Eleanor's son, the 10th Earl of Strathmore, revived the estate, remodelling the old house and completing the Chapel. His son, John Bowes, inherited Gibside, but not the title, as he had been born out of wedlock, and chose to live most of his life in France. However, he never forgot his roots, returning to be buried in the Chapel and founding the Bowes Museum at Barnard Castle. After John Bowes's death in 1885, Gibside went into a slow decline, as George Bowes's buildings decayed and the outlines of his vast garden became blurred by undergrowth. In 1974 the Chapel and the Long Walk were given to the National Trust, which has been gradually reuniting the historic core of the garden, so that 'the grandeur and magnificence of what Mr Bowes has done' can be enjoyed once more.

(Right) George Bowes, creator of the garden

(Far right) Mary Eleanor Bowes

TOUR OF THE GARDEN

The following tour describes Gibside as it was originally intended to be seen. Visitors currently arrive via the Watergate Entrance Drive (29), but the Trust hopes to reinstate the historical sequence.

THE APPROACH TO GIBSIDE

Historically, Gibside lay in the north-west of Co. Durham with the city of Durham as its administrative capital. The Bowes family had a town house near the cathedral in Durham's South Bailey, which was an asset when roads became impassable in bad weather. The town of Newcastle was much nearer to Gibside than Durham, but the River Tyne had precipitous banks, and until 1771 was crossed by only a single medieval bridge, which made access difficult. The original approach to Gibside was from the road to Whickham, the eastern boundary of the property.

CUT THORN FARM (1)

Cut Thorn Farm is situated near the Whickham road on the high land overlooking the rest of the estate. The farm was small and undeveloped until the 10th Earl of Strathmore began to construct buildings according to the new ideas of agricultural improvement current at the end of the eighteenth century. Good provision was made for the needs of animals, and the Fold, with a yard abutting West Lane, was particularly well planned. In the mid-nineteenth century it became the home farm to the Gibside estate; it was acquired by the National Trust in 1997.

THE WHICKHAM ENTRANCE DRIVE (2)

In the early eighteenth century the entrance drive led from the Whickham road, passing the houses at Hill Top, then curved round Cut Thorn Farm before descending steeply to reach Gibside House. For five years a waggonway cut across the drive carrying coal to the Tyne, before the 'War of the Waggon Ways' led to its abandonment (see p.23). The main entrance to Gibside was from the east for many years, but the building of the turnpike road along the Derwent Valley in 1833 led to a new drive being made leading to Rowlands Gill – the Watergate Entrance Drive (29).

SNIPES DENE (3)

The Gibside estate was divided between land that sloped and was suitable only for growing trees, and ground which could be used for arable crops. Snipes Dene is a narrow valley with ravine-like sides which contains trees similar to the original forest. In the 1780s Mary Eleanor's rascally second husband Stoney Bowes tried to sell Gibside timber without her consent, declaring that such wood could not be found elsewhere save in His Majesty's docks. The estate was renowned for its fine beech and oak. Coal was mined here early in the seventeenth century, and some of it may have been used to fire the Gibside Forge, situated on Warren Haugh. Early in the eighteenth century, Gibside coal was considered in London to be the best available. Today an adit, or entry to a mine, can be seen halfway down Snipes Dene near an earth bridge. It is located on the side of a coal seam and has a barrel-vaulted tunnel leading into the mine. Another entrance lower down the ravine has been blocked.

THE NEW COACH WAY (4)

When George Bowes started to lay out the estate in 1729, he wished to make a better approach. This was made possible when he foreclosed on the mortgage for Hollinside, the adjoining property, in 1735. The Hardings had owned Hollinside for 200 years, but in spite of coal deposits there, were much in debt. Bowes wrote to Mrs Verney, the mother of his first wife, that he had long wanted the property, 'as it will not only enlarge my possessions at this retired place, but will give me room to make new beauties by its happy situation'. As well as the purchase price, Bowes gave annuities to various members of the Harding family to recompense them for the loss of Hollinside.

The new drive was planned by William Joyce (active 1730–67), the head gardener at Gibside. It was built largely on steeply sloping ground, which meant that a great deal of earth had to be transported to construct it. The drive curved along the edge of Snipes Dene Wood with a large drop below. Double lodges were built in 1798–9 about 23 metres from the edge of the wood to mark the Gibside boundary. The lodges were single-storey with pyramidal roofs. There was a gate for pedestrians beside each lodge and a wide gate between them for carriages. Various entries were made to Fellside

The Banqueting House

road as the drive was extended through Hollinside Park. In the mid-eighteenth century these lodges were demolished and new double lodges, on a similar plan, were built near Clockburn Lane. These were of coursed ashlar (smoothly finished stone) with pointed arches to the doors and windows. The roofs were masked by crenellations on all sides save the rear. According to a tenancy agreement of 1902, the tenant had to attend to the lodge gates and assist in preventing trespass in the grounds. The lodges now form the entrance to Whickham Golf Course.

THE OUTER PLEASURE GROUNDS

THE BANQUETING HOUSE (5)

Many of George Bowes's garden buildings were located so they could be seen from the New Coach Way. The Banqueting House was situated on flat land high above the rest of the estate and itself formed a viewing point from which his improvements could be seen. Bowes chose Daniel Garrett (active 1727–53) as architect for the new buildings. Garrett was one of Lord Burlington's architectural assistants and often acted as his clerk of works. He set up a practice in the north of England and worked at Stanwick, Wallington and Castle Howard. Bowes's belvedere has a Gothick exterior with cinquefoil window heads and quatrefoil openings in the battlemented balustrade. Garrett also designed an elaborate plasterwork ceiling for the main room in a Gothick style, with a floral motif echoing medieval fan vaulting (now gone). Work began in 1741 and was completed in 1745.

Banqueting houses had been fashionable since Tudor times and were sometimes built on the roof of a mansion, as at Hardwick Hall in Derbyshire. Later they were placed in the grounds away from the house, and it was part of the enjoyment to explore the estate before arriving at the banqueting house. If there was no provision for cooking, the main part of the banquet would be held in the mansion and then the guests would be taken to the banqueting house, where wine and sweetmeats

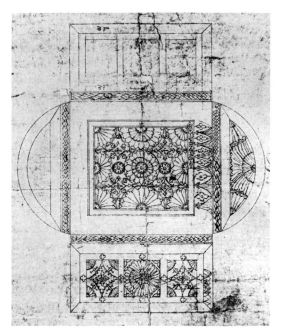

Daniel Garrett's design for the ceiling plasterwork of the Banqueting House

were served, the estate surveyed, and the company entertained. The plan of the Gibside Banqueting House was simple – a 9.8-metre-long Great Room for eating and drinking, behind which were a smaller ante-room and kitchen, each with its closet or cupboard. One of George Bowes's passions was music, and the Banqueting House also provided an ideal setting for concerts. From the west closet a ladder reached the roof from where panoramic views of the estate could be appreciated.

The Banqueting House is now owned by the Landmark Trust and is open only to visitors staying there.

THE OCTAGON POND (6)

The Octagon Pond, or New Bason, was begun in 1740, and lay at the foot of a wide ride below the Banqueting House. George Bowes visited the famous landscape gardens at Stowe in Buckinghamshire in 1737 and was much impressed by the Octagon Pond there. The Gibside pond and the overall layout of the garden were planned by

Stephen Switzer (1682–1745), a well-known authority on landscape design. His ideas bridged the transition between the formal garden and the informal landscape. He believed that estate management was more important than the enjoyment of gardens for their own sake, and that it led to the profitable and pleasurable appreciation of the countryside. The outlying fields of the estate became part of the gardens, with ha-has, or sunk fences, dividing them from the pleasure grounds. He also believed in water as an element in landscape. At Gibside the River Derwent formed the western boundary of the estate, while the Lily Pond (12) and the Octagon Pond provided water vistas for other parts of the garden. Switzer made a series of three banks overlooking the Octagon Pond where statues were displayed. The pond was described by Reinhold Angerstein, a Swede visiting the nearby Crowley Ironworks in 1754, as 'a pool according to the Greek taste, adorned with a number of statues'. Other earthworks gave variety to the vista below the Banqueting House, which was lined by a beech avenue in the nineteenth century. A reservoir was constructed in the mid-nineteenth century in the trees to the north-east of the Banqueting House; it supplied water for a fountain in the Octagon Pond.

THE STABLES (7)

When George Bowes first inherited Gibside in 1722, the Stables were to the west of Gibside House. He later moved them to the east of the mansion, but this position was also unsatisfactory, and he decided to make new stables away from the house. At that time most stables in the north-east of England were of a single range, as at Belsay Castle in Northumberland, but Bowes wanted something grander. The Stables were built to a design by Daniel Garrett on a courtyard plan. The building was fronted by a Palladian façade five bays wide, with the three central bays pedimented and projecting slightly. The façade overlooked the New Coach Way and could readily be appreciated by visitors. Wings on either side of the Palladian centrepiece were set back and had the appearance of pavilions, contrasting with the inner courtyard built in the Northumbrian vernacular style. The south side of the Stables

The Stables

was the main entrance and had two wooden doors. Another entrance on the west meant that a coach could enter through one gateway and leave through the other without having to reverse. Building began in 1747 and was largely complete by 1751. The stables are presently being restored by the National Trust.

THE ROUND POINT (8)

'Top of the Hollow Walk' was a point from which rides to the Lily Pond and the Banqueting House above the Octagon Pond could be viewed. To the north, the Column to Liberty (10) could be seen high above, and to the south was a view of the Chapel (27). In 1953 the woods at Gibside were leased to the Forestry Commission, which changed the alignment of the road, partially destroying this viewpoint. The Trust is presently restoring it.

THE HOLLOW WALK (9)

The Hollow Walk is a continuation of the Long Walk (24), which was completed in 1749, towards the Column to Liberty, which was finished in 1757, and so must have been created between these dates. The ground fell away steeply at the north-east end

of the Long Walk, and the broad dene below was crossed by streams from near to the Stables and the Octagon Pond. The streams were culverted and a great quantity of soil was moved to make a wide earth bridge. The lower ends of the culverts were reinforced by walls which were buttressed to retain the heavy weight of the earth in the Walk above. Many of George Bowes's labourers had experience in mining and were well used to earth-moving and building walls to retain it.

THE COLUMN TO LIBERTY (10)

Bowes liked to be original. Up to 1750 he had built a bath house (18) with plasterwork by the renowned Francesco Vassalli, a banqueting house with some of the earliest Gothic Revival decoration in the north, and stables on the fashionable courtyard plan. Now he wished to raise a column which would be second in height only to the Monument in London (62 metres). Daniel Garrett appears to have been the architect, and on his death in 1753, building ceased and scaffolding was removed. James Paine (1717–89) was called in, the scaffolding restored and building continued. Bowes visited John Cheere's stoneyard in London to seek ideas for a suitable statue to crown the column. At one time Minerva, goddess of Wisdom, was the choice, but in the end the figure of Liberty was chosen to proclaim Bowes's support for the Whig Party. The

9

statue was carved by Christopher Richardson (1709–81) of Doncaster and depicts a young woman dressed in a fashionable gown. In her right hand she holds a Staff of Maintenance and a Cap of Liberty (symbols also associated with Britannia), a fold of dress in her left, and looks down towards Gibside House. The statue was gilded with 66 books of gold leaf and surmounts a truly monumental Tuscan column, which dominates the lower Derwent Valley and can be seen from across the Tyne. Its height is over 40 metres, with a statue 3.8 metres high. From the foot of the column a panoramic view could be seen of the estate and the river valley. The Trust restored the column and statue in 1993.

THE BRICK KILN FIELD (11)

Estates in the eighteenth century tried to be as self-sufficient as possible. Brick kilns were sometimes built near the site of an intended building, and at Gibside the making of bricks was concentrated in a large field on the high ground near the Column to Liberty. There are still the remains of the pond where the clay was soaked before being put into moulds and fired. There must also have been sheds for drying the bricks. In spite of frequent ploughing, the Brick Kiln Field is still covered in small pieces of brick, and more rise to the surface each year. Other materials for building were produced on the spot. On the Gibside estate there are the remains of at least six quarries, and others belonging to George Bowes were situated nearby.

THE LILY POND (12)

The Lily Pond, or Old Bason, was part of Switzer's layout for Gibside, and a semicircular bank to the north-west of the pond was contoured with his characteristic ramps. Work began in 1734, and tree-planting was undertaken in 1737, with walks above the pond being made two years later.

The Lily Pond was the point from which four rides began. The one to the north led to Lady Haugh (14) and the River Derwent, that to the west crossed the upper part of Lady Haugh before it reached the river, while the ride to the east focused on the Column to Liberty. The ride to the south joined a drive from the Octagon Pond.

*The Column
to Liberty*

The south front of Gibside House

Originally the Lily Pond was centrally situated with the road dividing in two to pass round it. The Forestry Commission found the road unsuitable for removing felled trees and altered its route. This meant that the lines of some vistas were destroyed or were no longer easily seen. The National Trust is working to restore these views.

THE LIME WALK (13)

The Lime Walk was concealed by Forestry Commission planting. Until recently there was no known record of its existence, but its position was shown on a second edition Ordnance Survey map annotated for military purposes in 1942. The ride crossing the Lily Pond from the north-east to south-west was lined with lime trees. Limes were sometimes pollarded or, as Switzer recounts, cut into a conical shape. Stumps of the old trees remain, and the Trust has begun to replace the limes.

LADY HAUGH (14)

The Lime Walk led from the Lily Pond to the lower end of Lady Haugh. Downstream from Lady Haugh one of the early Gibside mills was situated with the mill leet cutting across the water meadow.

George Bowes tried to make it a profitable venture by converting it from a corn mill to a paper mill. The mill continued to function until 1780, when Stoney Bowes destroyed it after a quarrel with the miller.

THE INNER PLEASURE GROUNDS

GIBSIDE HOUSE (15)

The present Gibside House was built by William and Jane Blakiston from 1603 to 1620. It stands on a shelf overlooking the River Derwent on a site that had already been used for at least one house. The three-storey Jacobean house was an imposing building with mullioned windows lighting the main rooms.

When George Bowes came into possession of Gibside, he had a fortune large enough to afford a succession of garden buildings, but the uncertainties of the coal trade meant a new house was impossible. His two marriages to heiresses did not provide the sum needed to build afresh and he may have preferred the existing Jacobean mansion to a fashionable new Palladian house.

However, Bowes and each of his successors altered the large and rambling building. Bowes added fourteen sash-windows, moved the kitchen from the west to the east end of the house, and provided that new necessity, a library. His daughter, Mary Eleanor, added another wing in an attempt to improve the kitchen offices. Her interest in botany may have prompted her to plant 'Mr. Wilmers great double daffodill' in clumps along the edge of the terrace north of the house. This striking daffodil, with its centre petals folded like a carnation, lay dormant until the land was recently cleared, when it flowered once again.

Bowes's grandson, the 10th Earl of Strathmore, again tried to improve the kitchens, and Fryer's estate map of 1803 shows a spacious domestic court to the east of the house. He also removed the top storey, replacing it with a colossal parapet with cross-loops in 1803–10. John Dobson (1787–1865) drew up plans in 1814 to alter the house and add a two-storey wing containing an orangery, but they were not implemented. The 10th Earl seems to have preferred to bring up his son, John Bowes, at Streatlam, the family seat near Barnard Castle.

Later the house was lived in by John Bowes's mother, the Countess of Strathmore, and her second husband, Sir William Hutt. After his wife's death in 1860, Sir William renewed the lease of Gibside but later decided to retire to the Isle of Wight. Following John Bowes's death in 1885, Gibside and his other properties in England reverted to his uncle, the 13th Earl of Strathmore, who lived mainly in Scotland and Hertfordshire. Part of Gibside House was rented out to a private tenant, but efforts to let it as a hydropathic establishment were unsuccessful. As late as 1917 there were plans to lease the house to Durham Education Committee. During the First World War land girls lived there, and it was used as a Home Guard store during the Second World War. After roof tiles were removed in the 1950s, decay was rapid and now only the shell survives. This was becoming increasingly dangerous, so a programme of consolidation began in 2002 and is ongoing.

GUNNER'S WALK (16)

Gunner's Walk was so called because of the statue of a gunner taking aim which once stood half-concealed on the river bank. It may have been the work of John Cheere, who produced cast-lead sculptures to be placed in landscape settings. The figure was painted by an estate worker in 1753. George Bowes's first-known visit to John Cheere's sculpture yard was in 1756, when he was looking for a figure to crown the Column to Liberty, but he may have bought the gunner on a previous visit.

The Walk led from the Bath House (18) to Lady Haugh (14). It was engineered across a steep gradient near the Bath House, crossing two small ravines and then following the river line by Lady Haugh. Since 1733 retaining walls had been built along the Gibside bank of the River Derwent 1.5 metres high and 1 metre deep and made from carefully cut stone blocks of almost ashlar quality. The Derwent was liable to sudden flooding and the wall was to protect a mile and a half of the Gibside boundary from Leap Mill Burn on the west of the estate downstream to the Paper Mill. This wall can be seen from the other side of the river and, in restored form, on the banks of Lady Haugh.

THE GREEN CLOSE (17)

The Green Close was an area of land between two streams leading to Gunner's Walk. Here George Bowes's twelve-year-old daughter, Mary Eleanor, had her first garden in 1761, when the estate joiner was 'Palisading Miss Bowes's Garden in the Green Close'. It was just far enough away from the house to provide a challenge and it furthered her love of botany. The Close was an open space for much of the estate's history, and during the nineteenth century a mound here was crowned by a large stone basin to provide a feature for a walk near Gibside House. A plantation of conifers on the Green Close was removed in 2005, and the area will once more be returned to a grassy lawn.

THE BATH HOUSE (18)

The Bath House was the first of George Bowes's garden buildings. At Gibside he followed the example of Lord Burlington, who on returning from the Grand Tour in 1717 designed and built a bath house at Chiswick. Building began in 1733, and by 1736 its decoration was complete.

It was situated on a shelf cut across a slope that became cliff-like below the building. A vertical wall retained the site, 18 metres above the River Derwent. It was a single-storey classical building of three rooms with a recessed portico. The interior was decorated by Francesco Vassalli, a well-known stuccoist who went on to decorate the Temple of the Four Winds at Castle Howard in Yorkshire. Bath houses were very fashionable at the time, and cold baths in particular were thought to be healthy. There appears to have been a plunge bath, each of the rooms had a fireplace, and there was provision for card-playing, which seems to have been its main use. By 1827 the roof had collapsed and in 1854 the building was engulfed in a landslip which made repair impossible. Gradually, its stones were removed for use in other buildings, and now only the partly excavated foundations remain.

THE BATH HOUSE DENE WALKS (19)

Walking was one of the favoured recreations of those living at Gibside. George Bowes asked his head gardener, William Joyce, to lay out the walks, and his garden buildings were intended to give them added interest. Walks were cut through the flat wooded area above the Bath House. One path led down the dene to the Bath. The Bath House Well was situated nearby and was perhaps its source of water. On the estate map made at the time of Mary Eleanor Bowes's marriage to the 9th Earl of Strathmore in 1767, nineteen Gibside walks were shown.

THE ICE-HOUSE (20)

The Ice-house was situated above the stream leading to the Bath House, as the slope gave good drainage. The Ice-house has now been robbed of its original thatched roof and some of its insulating earth. The entry door leads to a passage 1.5 metres long with another door immediately before the chamber. It is of an inverted beehive construction made of rosy red brick, 5.5 metres deep and approximately 8 metres across. The top of the structure is a brick groin vault with cross arches on either side of the entrance. Labourers would fill the cavity with ice in the winter months and this would gradually be used during the summer.

THE ORANGERY (21)

Mary Eleanor Bowes was described as 'the most

The Bath House in 1827; drawing by Martha Helen Davidson

(Above)
The Orangery

(Left)
The Orangery in
1827; drawing by
Martha Helen
Davidson

(Opposite)
The Long Walk

intelligent female botanist' of her time. When the Chapel was weatherfast, though not fully decorated, she began to make an imposing greenhouse. The architect is not known, though it is in the style of James Paine, who designed the Chapel. Building started in 1772 and took three years. The Green House, as it was then called, was built on a rectangular podium with a canted bay at the rear, and measured 18.2 × 12.4 metres. It was faced in ashlar stone from quarries on or near the estate. Brick was used in the interior, with a lath-and-plaster finish. The tall windows fronting the building looked out on the Green House Close, where an ornamental pond 15 metres across was dug, while at the rear of the building smaller windows were chosen because of its northern aspect and exposed position. The arcade had seven bays of Tuscan columns and led to the largest room. Small lobbies at the rear formed spaces to keep the temperature even for the rooms housing Mary Eleanor's collection of exotic plants. A balustrade partly hid the hipped roof and was decorated with ornamental urns. Orange trees were placed in the seven windows of the arcade to mark its completion.

In 1855 Mary Eleanor's grandson, John Bowes, converted the greenhouse into a fashionable conservatory. The hipped slate roof was altered to six pitches of glass supported by a row of iron columns, and a large planter was created from eighteenth-century bricks in the centre of the building. Today the urns which used to adorn the top of the Orangery have disappeared and the building is ruinous. The columns have, however, been stabilised, and further restoration and repairs to the fabric of the building are proceeding.

WALLED GARDEN (22)

George Bowes decided to move the vegetable garden away from Gibside House and in 1734 began building new garden walls. The walls took two years to complete and enclosed an area of just over 3½ acres (1.4 hectares). There was a D-shaped pond in the corner nearest Gibside House with tree-lined walks laid out between the vegetable plots. Hot beds, deep pits filled with bark and manure, were used for forcing plants. Later a series of glasshouses was built to provide fruit out of season. In the 1830s extensive vineries were built and an Orchid House was added by John Bowes.

THE GARDEN HOUSE (23)

The Garden House was built for the head gardener overlooking the Walled Garden so that he could protect valuable fruit and vegetables against thieves and vandals. Georgian in origin, the house was at one time two dwellings and has been altered considerably. It is of two storeys, with sash-windows and a single-storey extension.

THE LONG WALK (24)

The Long Walk or Avenue was part of Switzer's

The Chapel from the east

plan for Gibside, though it was rather old-fashioned by the time it was begun in 1746. The Long Walk is just under half a mile long and cuts across the sloping ground of the estate. Above the Walk much earth was cut away and stabilised, with a ha-ha between the fields and the Walk. On the other side the ground fell away. Elms were brought from Lumley Cassle to line the sides of the avenue. Before the trees grew, much of the estate could be seen from the Long Walk. The broad grassy avenue not only provided a suitably grand focus to George Bowes's landscape garden, but also gave him somewhere to exercise his bloodstock.

The Gibside sketchbook of 1827 shows the Long Walk without trees on the Park Fields side of the avenue and a plantation of trees on the other side. A later hand has titled the drawing 'The Racecourse', and perhaps John Bowes's four Derby winners

were also exercised here. Today double avenues of Turkey oaks with some sycamore line the sides of the Long Walk.

PARK FIELDS (25)

The three Park Fields together form the most productive part of the estate. The land slopes down towards the river until it reaches the sunk fence of the Long Walk. Near the Chapel the woods project into Hunters Meadow, with twin streams and their confluence hidden by trees. There is a reservoir in the middle field with tree-lined banks. Single oaks and small groups preserve the park effect.

THE WEST WOOD WAY (26)

The West Wood Way was begun in 1749, before the building of the Column to Liberty. It started from the Stables, crossing a ride from the Octagon Pond, and then skirted the Hall Field until the West

Wood was reached. The line of the Leap Mill Burn was followed until it joined the bridle path to the neighbouring property of Friarside. A small ha-ha protected the wood from straying cattle. The construction took two years and was perhaps the last of the circuits planned by Switzer.

A series of bell-pits can be seen in the West Wood, and nearby the largest of the Gibside quarries looks as if it could still produce usable stone.

THE CHAPEL (27)

George Bowes had wanted to build a chapel in the 1730s to commemorate the death of his first wife after only two and a half months of marriage. This intention was not fulfilled, and in his will of 1750 he resolved to erect a chapel which was to contain his mausoleum, but to delay construction until after his death. Bowes's health was failing in 1759, when he finally decided to begin work. James Paine, who had completed the Column to Liberty and done some decoration at Gibside House, was chosen as architect.

The plan of the Chapel is a Greek cross within a square, with the eastern side flattened to form the entrance. Six giant engaged Ionic columns line this façade with a portico of four principal columns. Steps lead up to a podium above the mausoleum, on which the Chapel stands. The delicate carving of the capitals, friezes and modillions under the portico is worthy of the sculptor Christopher Richardson. A shallow dome surmounts a tall drum, which is decorated with festoons of flowers. The height of the drum was necessary so that the dome could be seen in a near view. The interior of the Chapel has a Georgian simplicity, which on further inspection reveals a more complex form. Composite columns support the crossings and the central dome, while engaged Ionic pilasters bear the smaller and lower domes in each corner. The space is lit by Diocletian windows high in the end walls of the transepts and by round-headed windows in the corner bays.

At the rear, double iron doors at the foot of a gaunt wall protect the entrance to the mausoleum, which was made of the same local creamy sandstone as the rest of the Chapel. A short passage and some steps lead to the circular burial vault, which is

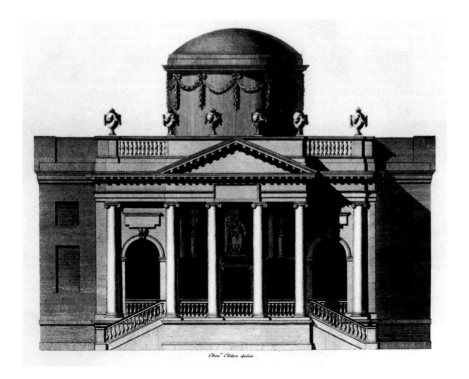

The entrance front of the Chapel; engraving from James Paine's Plans, Elevations, Sections … *(1767)*

The interior of the Chapel; engraving from Paine's Plans, Elevations, Sections ... *(1767)*

8.5 metres in diameter and 3 metres high, with eleven niches. The vault was built of concentric rings of fine masonry. George Bowes's body was interred in Whickham church until work was completed on the vault, which then became his final resting place.

When the 10th Earl of Strathmore decided to finish the Chapel, its decoration had been completed up to the cornice. The elaborate coffering of the dome and ceiling alcoves shown in James Paine's section of the Chapel was not carried out. Instead the ribs of the ceiling vaults were decorated with stucco, which outlined the ceiling panels. The plasterwork was begun in 1811 and was still being carried out in 1812, when the Chapel was consecrated; it was completed only in 1816.

The furnishings include a three-decker pulpit made of cherrywood, with a sounding board supported by an Ionic column and a staircase on each side. The preacher used the top pulpit; readings were given from the middle; a clerk sat at the bottom. In front of it is the railed-off altar. Square box pews were provided in the corners for the owner, agent and chaplain, with curved seats for the servants and visitors. The appearance of the Chapel has changed little since it was finished.

THE CHAPLAIN'S HOUSE (28)

The Chaplain's House was built in 1813–14 as a modest dwelling for the chaplain attending Gibside Chapel. The façade towards the Chapel is of three bays of ashlar with a hipped slate roof. An extension was added at the rear in 1975 to make the house suitable for the family of the Chapel Keeper.

The interior of the Chapel is dominated by the early nineteenth-century three-decker pulpit

THE WATERGATE ENTRANCE DRIVE (29)

In the eighteenth century this coal-mining area of Durham was crossed by waggonways, but roads were largely neglected until the advent of turnpike roads. The opening of the chain bridge across the Tyne at Scotswood in 1831 made it easier to get from Gibside to Newcastle, and in 1833 an Act of Parliament was passed to build a turnpike road from Axwell Park to Shotley Bridge. One advocate of this road along the Derwent Valley was the 22-year-old John Bowes, who had inherited the 10th Earl's English properties, and owned a plantation affected by it.

In 1855 Bowes wrote in his memorandum book about opening up the road across Warren Haugh on the west of his estate to give easier access to Gibside House. He was an infrequent visitor to Gibside at this time, but must have seen that this new turnpike road would benefit the estate. A new railway was built in 1867 along the Derwent Valley to reach Blackhill, near Consett. John Bowes refused to let the railway pass along the southern bank of the Derwent through the main Gibside policies. Instead, the railway passed through Goodshields Haugh, the northern part of Hollinside Park, crossing the river on an imposing nine-arched viaduct to reach the station at Rowlands Gill. It re-crossed the River Derwent on another tall viaduct avoiding the western end of the Gibside estate. This offered a more convenient way of transporting timber and other produce of the estate, as well as taking passengers across the Tyne to Newcastle.

At this time Leap Mill Burn was the boundary of the Gibside estate, the land between the Burn and Busty Bank Road belonging to the Marquess of Bute. So when the new road had been engineered, a new lodge was built within the Gibside boundary on the east bank of the Burn. Watergate Lodge was L-shaped, of two storeys, and overlooked Warren Haugh to the north and the Chapel high above in the trees to the east. What had formerly been a bridle path to Friarside became the main entrance to the estate, and it remains the entrance for present-day visitors.

THE WIDER ESTATE

A survey of 1706 gave the size of Gibside estate as 1,516 acres (613.5 hectares). It was a time when farming and rents from tenants no longer gave the landowner a good living, and many landowners in the north-east mined coal on their own property. When George Bowes inherited Gibside in 1722, the estate had become run down under the former owners, the Blakiston family. Sir Francis Blakiston, Bowes's grandfather, had little business acumen and leased the profitable Gibside mining rights in 1692 to the Hon. Charles Montagu rather than exploit them himself.

As well as being an astute man of business, Bowes, like his eldest brother William, was highly acquisitive. He bought land adjoining his Gibside estate, and any property nearby that might one day be linked up with his possessions. He also acquired land with exploitable mineral rights. One nearby property, Bird Hill, was bought by his elder brother Thomas in 1722 during the six months that he owned Gibside. Later, Bird Hill became the dower house for Gibside. In 1804 the 10th Earl of Strathmore paid for 'making the new Road and Pleasure Grounds before Bird Hill House' in preparation for his sister and her daughters going to live there.

John Bowes and his Strathmore successors lived mostly away from Gibside, and although they invested in the estate, they increasingly sold off outlying parts of it, until by the 1970s it had shrunk to less than half its original size.

Gibside from the north-west in 1782

THE OWNERS OF GIBSIDE

EARLY HISTORY

High above the water meadows of Lady Haugh on the east bank of the River Derwent stand the roofless ruins of Gibside House, the core of which was built between 1603 and 1620 for William and Jane Blakiston. An inventory taken in 1608 suggests that the three-storey Jacobean building was already comfortably furnished: the old parlour contained 'one paire of Virginalls', the new parlour 'two carpetts of blewe and green'.

In August 1693 Gibside passed to the Bowes family with the marriage of the Blakistons' great-granddaughter Elizabeth to Sir William Bowes of Streatlam Castle, his ancestral home 40 miles to the south of Gibside near Barnard Castle. One of the few surviving reminders of this period is the Bowes Cup, which is hallmarked for 1675 and so is the earliest known gold racing cup in Britain, testifying to the family's passion for horse-racing; it is now in the Victoria & Albert Museum. In the space of twelve years, Elizabeth produced ten children, eight of whom survived infancy. After Sir William died in 1706 at the age of 50, she was left to manage the Gibside and Streatlam estates until their eldest son, another William, came of age.

William Blakiston Bowes (1696/7–1721) was about nine when his father died. Like several other members of the family, he caught smallpox, which marked his face and hands for life and hindered his efforts to find a rich wife, whom he specified should be 'of a modest discreet behaviour not deformed'. William himself was a difficult young man, who did not get on with his mother. When she tried to get him to come up to Gibside from London in 1718, he replied: 'Surely you don't think me such a fool to prefer the Charms of a stupid, dull, Country Life, to

(Right) The porch of Gibside House bears the coat of arms of William Blakiston and his and his wife Jane's initials, with the date 1625, below the royal arms of James I

the pleasure of the Town', but went on, 'the addition of £1500 per annum to my Estate, if You will find me any such advantageous proffer in Your Country, I will willingly set out to Morrow'.

When he came into his estate in 1717, William made the Grand Tour to Venice and Padua in the company of the Scottish portrait painter and dealer Andrew Hay. On his return, he began rebuilding Streatlam Castle in French style: it 'will be the best in our Northern parts', he wrote in 1720. He prob-

ably also commissioned the superb silver-gilt sideboard dish and ewer made by David Willaume in 1718 and engraved with the quartered Bowes arms. He died unmarried and intestate in 1721, leaving Gibside to his younger brother, Thomas, who had 'an uncertain temper, which does not suffer him to agree with anybody'. Thomas, however, died six months later, and the estate passed to the third brother, George, who was to transform it over the next 40 years.

GEORGE BOWES (1701–60)

He's about six foot in Height,
Wo[ul]d he walk but upright...
His complexion is good...
His Mouth & Nose small...
His Eyes grey as a cat
Hansom Legs, Autre Chose,
And his Name is George Bowes.

According to his daughter, George Bowes was a great rake in his youth. Certainly, he shared his brothers' hot temper, fighting a duel with an equally fiery local landowner in 1726. He loved gambling, dancing, food and drink: among the rooms in Gibside House was a 'Sotts Hall'. He introduced fox-hunting to Co. Durham and developed his father's stud at Streatlam. But he also enjoyed more intellectual pleasures.

Bowes played the harpsichord and invited the Whickham Strollers to perform at Gibside at Christmas. He commissioned portraits of himself and his family from Enoch Seeman, one of Hogarth's lesser rivals, and spent 1,500 guineas on a Rubens. Before he came into his inheritance, he had served in the regiment of General George Wade, whose London house was designed by Lord Burlington, the pioneer of the Palladian movement. Burlington may have introduced Bowes to Daniel Garrett, the architect of the Stables and probably also of the Column to Liberty, who was working as his assistant in the early 1720s. Garrett was also a protégé of Bowes's old friend and neighbour at Rokeby Park, the amateur architect Sir Thomas Robinson. Bowes certainly subscribed to the major architectural publications of the time, such as William Kent's *Designs of Inigo Jones* (1727), James Gibbs's *Book of Architecture* (1728) and Isaac Ware's 1738 edition of Palladio.

TAKING COALS TO NEWCASTLE

George Bowes was not just a hard-living and cultured landowner. He was also a ruthlessly successful businessman, who earned the nicknames 'the Count' and 'the Czar'. The source of his wealth and power was coal. William Blakiston Bowes had begun to exploit the rich coal and iron deposits on the estate, having realised the crucial importance of better transport links between his pits and the quays on the River Tyne. In April 1721, shortly before his death, William had written: 'last Monday, we began to lead the new Waggon Way, which is the beginning of my profitt; it is a work of such importance & crosses so many Mountains & Vales which are all levelled, that I can compare it to nothing more properly than to the Via Appia [the main road into Rome].' It is significant that George Bowes's first building project, in 1725, was to construct the Causey Arch across the Causey Burn to carry waggons of his coal down to the Tyne. From there it was transported by a Newcastle 'fitter' down river to Tynemouth, where it was loaded into a collier, which carried it to the Port of London, where it was unloaded by the London lightermen and finally sold by the coal-merchants of the Woodmongers Company. This long and complex chain ate into the profits of the original producers like Bowes. So in June 1725 he met two fellow Durham coal-owners, George Liddell and Charles Atkinson, in Newcastle to found the Grand Alliance. They agreed to bury their differences – differences that had been exacerbated by Bowes's hot temper – and form a price-fixing cartel. Bowes became the effective boss of the Grand Alliance and further bolstered his position through political office. He was Whig MP for Co. Durham from 1727 until his death, and mayor of Hartlepool and Durham on numerous occasions, but despite building a new school and laying out substantial sums in election bribes, he failed to make any headway in Newcastle, which was ruled by the Tories.

Bowes sought to increase his status still further by

his marriage in October 1724 to Eleanor Verney, the granddaughter and heiress of Lord Willoughby de Broke of Compton Verney in Warwickshire. Although Eleanor was only fourteen, this seems to have been a love match. In July 1724 he had written to her: 'I am not able to bear the cruel absence from my Angel any longer without haveing recourse to Pen & Paper for relief of my tortured Heart which can at present find no other way to ease its self.' Eleanor was also something of a child prodigy – 'the most accomplished of her sex', he called her. He was consequently grief-stricken when she died in January 1725. Lady Mary Wortley Montagu took a more cynical view:

Hail happy bride, for thou are truly blest!
Three months of rapture, crown'd with endless rest.

George Bowes (1701–60), the creator of the Gibside gardens; by Enoch Seeman, 1744 (Strathmore Estates, Glamis Castle)

The Column to Liberty and Gibside House from across the Derwent Valley

CREATING THE GARDEN

Eleanor died before she came into her inheritance. Bowes was also laying out large sums on enlarging the estate and developing his coal-mines. He could, therefore, afford to build only out of income, which was heavily dependent on the unpredictable economic cycle. For this reason, perhaps, he decided not to remodel the Jacobean Gibside House in a more fashionable style. His ambitious plans for the garden also had to be implemented gradually over three decades, with each of the new garden buildings being put up over four to five years by his own estate workers, aided by specialist craftsmen for the decoration.

Bowes began planting on a large scale in 1729, and two years later paid Stephen Switzer £10 'for drawing a Plann of Gardens, Plantations, Green Close &c.' Alas, this plan has disappeared, for Switzer was one of the most interesting garden designers and nurserymen of the early eighteenth century, who had already worked at Castle Howard and Blenheim. He seems to have devised the basic structure from which the garden developed. It consisted of long straight walks near the house (what Switzer called his 'boldest Strokes') and more circuitous subsidiary paths, encircled by a drive from which broader views of the Derwent Valley landscape could be enjoyed. Switzer favoured water features and may have been responsible for proposing the Octagon Pond, which was dug in 1740–1. The first new building to go up was the Bath House overlooking the Derwent, in 1733–40. The mammoth brick walls of the Kitchen Garden were laid in 1734–6. The Gothick Banqueting House followed in 1741–5, which was placed at the head of a vista overlooking the Octagon Pond. This in turn is set above a key point where the West Wood Way joins the main drive to the house.

Bowes did not marry again for another eighteen years, until 1743; his second wife was Mary Gilbert, the heiress to St Paul's Walden Bury in Hertfordshire. Her father, Edward Gilbert, had built this beautiful house and laid out the garden there with rides through trees, and Bowes copied the idea at Gibside, naming one of his rides after Gilbert. Mary seems to have had an improving effect on the household: the Gaming Room became the Prayer Room. She also – at last – brought him an heir, named Mary Eleanor after his two wives.

In 1745 Bowes raised a cavalry regiment to

Within the park Bowes created a northern arcadia, but beyond, the effects of his mining activities were less pretty, as William Hutchinson acknowledged in his *History of Durham* (1787):

The adjacent country wears an unpleasant aspect to the traveller, cut and harrowed up with loaded carriages, scattered over with mean cottages, from whence swarm innumerable inhabitants, maintained by working in the mines; where many a sooty face is seen by every hedge-way side.

Bowes turned to another Palladian architect, James Paine, for his last and most ambitious garden building, the Chapel, which closes the southern end of the Long Walk. Paine had already completed the Column to Liberty after Garrett's death in 1753 and had carried out work on the house. The Chapel is Paine's only free-standing religious building and one of the masterpieces of the Palladian movement. Inspired by Palladio's Villa Rotonda in the Veneto, he adopted a Greek cross plan, with an Ionic portico facing the Long Walk, and a high central drum topped by a shallow dome. The Chapel was intended not only as a place of worship, but also as a family mausoleum with a handsome vaulted crypt beneath. Work started in November 1759, but little more than the crypt had been completed by the time Bowes died in September 1760, and it was left to his widow and executors to make the building weathertight. Fitting it out had to wait another 40 years.

defend Co. Durham when the Young Pretender and his Jacobite army marched south to stake a claim to the throne. He also presented the Duke of Cumberland with a horse on which he rode to Newcastle as he pursued the Jacobites back north towards Culloden. Bowes reaffirmed his loyalty to the Hanoverian regime and to the Whigs in 1750–7 by erecting the Column to Liberty, topped with a gilded female figure almost 4 metres high symbolising Liberty. The column closes the northern end of the Long Walk, which had been laid out in 1746–9 and which became the spine of the inner garden, providing views to the south from its broad raised terrace. The column was probably the final work at Gibside of Daniel Garrett, who in 1747–51 had built a handsome new stable block in the Palladian style to replace stables nearer the house. By now, Gibside was beginning to draw appreciative visitors, such as Spencer Cowper, Dean of Durham, who wrote in 1753:

Last week I was at Glory Bowes' at Gibside, to do it justice, I think it will be one of the finest places in the North when he has finish'd his design. The whole of his works takes in a range of seven miles; which if ever compleated will be worthy his Magnificence and Immensity.

'THE UNHAPPY COUNTESS' MARY ELEANOR BOWES (1749–1800)

George Bowes was almost 50 when his daughter, Mary Eleanor, was born. From the first, he treated her as an adult, perhaps in memory of his precocious first wife, but also because he may have realised that she was to be his only heir. At three she was vaccinated against smallpox, which had killed her uncle John. At four she could read well; by six she was having drawing and dancing lessons. She showed a particular aptitude for foreign languages and botany, being given her own garden, which was fenced off from the Green Close in 1761.

Mary Eleanor was considered by the blue-stocking Mrs Montagu 'really a fine girl, lively, sensible, and very civil and good natured'. But she was also an heiress worth £600,000, and as such, a constant prey to fortune-hunters, who took advantage of her good nature. She was courted by the great Whig politician Charles James Fox, and more successfully by John Lyon, 9th Earl of Strathmore, who was known as 'the Beautiful Strathmore'. But Mary Eleanor's mother did not approve of the match, complaining of 'disorder in the family; a mother, and many brothers and sisters, whom, perhaps, I should find troublesome; and lastly (the chief with her) his being a Scotchman'. This last was no objection to Mary Eleanor, who declared that she 'had a much greater partiality for the Scotch and Irish than for the English'.

By the time the complex marriage settlement, which obliged the 9th Earl to change his family name to Bowes Lyon, had been agreed, Mary

Mary Eleanor Bowes (1749–1800), 'the Unhappy Countess'; by J. C. D. Engleheart after George Engleheart, c.1765 (Bowes Museum)

Eleanor was herself beginning to have doubts: 'I found that our temperaments, dispositions and turns differed'. According to Jesse Foot, the family's doctor, who was later to write her sad story, the 9th Earl was 'not exactly calculated to make even a good learned woman a pleasing husband. His Lordship's pursuits were always innocent and without the smallest guile, but they were not of science or any other splendid quality. A sincere friend, a hearty Scotchman and a good bottle companion were parts of his character.' Mary Eleanor wanted to call off the wedding, but, as she herself admitted, was too proud to do so.

They were married On 24 February 1767 (her eighteenth birthday) at the most fashionable church in London, St George's, Hanover Square. Her wedding dress cost £3,000, and she wore a diamond stomacher worth £10,000 When their first child, Maria Jane, was born in April 1768, the bells rang out in celebration at Gibside. (A son, John, followed in 1769, and in all there were to be five children, the last born in 1773.) There were further celebrations at Gibside, when Mary Eleanor came of age in 1770:

An ox was roasted whole, which with other victuals and some hogsheads of strong ale &c., were given to the populace, many hundreds having assembled there to celebrate the day. The house was open for ten days to all persons who chose to repair thither to regale themselves.

But the couple themselves were far from happy. Both became ill, and the Earl gambled. In 1772–4 Mary Eleanor sank large sums more productively into the Green House, or Orangery, at Gibside for her exotic plants, but was accused by her husband of 'folly and extravagance such as the purchase of stuffed animals and other useless and absurd extravagances'. During the same period she remodelled the east wing of the house to provide better servants' quarters, and built a new bakehouse, dairy and laundry.

In 1769 Mary Eleanor published a bleak poem, *The Siege of Jerusalem*, about the torments of unrequited love. For she had fallen in love with James Graham, 'quite a boy, but a very extraordinary one', who then abandoned her: 'I thought he used me very ill' was her sad comment. In 1774 George

John Lyon, 9th Earl of Strathmore (1737–76); by Nathaniel Dance, 1762 (Strathmore Estates, Glamis Castle)

Grey began courting her, and finally in February 1776 seduced her: 'One unfortunate evening, I was off my guard, and ever after that I lived occasionally with him as his wife'. A fortnight later, the Earl, who was suffering from TB, sailed for the warmer climate of Lisbon in search of a cure, but died at sea. The Countess did not hear the news until April, when his last letter was delivered. Written when he knew he was dying, it is full of helpful, but rather cold-blooded, advice about how to manage the estate after his death, and concludes: 'I will say nothing of your extreme rage for literary fame. I think your own understanding, when matured, will convince you of the futility of the pursuit.'

Mary Eleanor was now able to indulge her passions, both intellectual and physical, to the full. According to Foot, she was 'the most intelligent female botanist of the age'. She bought Stanley House (later the home of Sir William Hamilton) near the Physic Garden in Chelsea. There she built greenhouses and conservatories, which she filled with exotic plants from all parts of the world. She

also became friends with Daniel Carl Solander, a Swedish botanist who had travelled to the South Pacific with Captain Cook.

In 1776 she became pregnant by Grey, and despite her behaviour becoming the subject of heated correspondence in the *Morning Post*, was about to marry him, when Andrew Robinson Stoney appeared on the scene. Stoney was an Irish adventurer, who was to be the model for the rogue-hero of Thackeray's novel, *The Memoirs of Barry Lyndon*. Foot has left vivid descriptions of both Stoney and Mary Eleanor:

His speech was soft, his height more than five feet ten, his eyes bright and small, he had a perfect command over them, his eye brows were low, large and sandy, his hair light, and his complexion muddy, his smile was agreeable, his wit ready, but he was always the first to laugh at what he said, which forced others to laugh also.

The Countess at this time was scarcely thirty years of age: she possessed a very pleasing embonpoint; her breast was uncommonly fine; her stature was rather

Andrew Robinson Stoney Bowes (d.1810); by John Downman (Fitzwilliam Museum, Cambridge)

ANDREW ROBINSON BOWES Esq.ʳ as he appeared in the Court of Kings Bench, on Tuesday the 28.ᵗʰ Nov. 1786. to answer the Articles exhibited against him, by his Wife, the Countess of Strathmore. Pubᵈ Decʳ 2.ᵈ 1786. by E. Jackson, Mary bone Street Golden Square.

*Stoney Bowes feigned injury at his court appearance on
28 November 1786. Mary Eleanor stands at the far right in
this contemporary caricature by James Gillray*

under the middle class; her hair brown; her eyes light,
small, and she was near sighted; her face was round;
her neck and shoulders graceful; her lower jaw rather
under-hanging, and which, whenever she was
agitated, was moved very uncommonly, as if convul-
sively, from side to side; her fingers were small, and
her hands were exceedingly delicate. She appeared in
very fine health; her complexion was particularly
clear; her dress displayed her person, it was elegant and
loose; she glowed with all the warmth of a gay widow,
about to be married.

Stoney won Mary Eleanor's heart by offering to
fight a duel with the editor of the *Morning Post*.
What she did not know was that in all probability
Stoney had written both sides of the correspondence himself; and that he was also already married.

Despite this, the couple were married in London on
17 January 1777. In accordance with George Bowes's
will, Stoney took the name of Bowes. He should
then have been able to get his hands on all the lucra-
tive revenues from her estates at Gibside and Streatlam. But he discovered to his horror that a week
before the marriage Mary Eleanor had secretly
drawn up an 'Ante-Nuptual Trust', which reserved
these estates and their income 'for her separate and
peculiar use and disposal, exclusive of any husband
she should thereafter marry with'. Stoney Bowes
was furious and proceeded to treat his wife with
miserable cruelty, extorting from her the written
Confessions in which she admitted to her past misbe-
haviour in graphic detail. Foot found her 'wonder-
fully ALTERED and DEJECTED. She was pale and
nervous, and her underjaw constantly moved from
side to side. If she said anything, she looked at
Bowes first.' To pay his gambling debts, he cut
down much valuable timber at Gibside, but no one

would buy it. He then sold her house in Chelsea, and proved equally tyrannical towards the Gibside tenants, as a contemporary verse complained:

Her Ladyship's tenants first gained his attention,
Whose treatment was cruel – most shocking to
    mention;
He rais'd all their rents, which if they could not pay,
He crav'd them, and seized them, then turned
    them away.
The helpless dependants – the labouring poor,
He removed from their work, or horse-whipp'd
    from his door.

By February 1785 Mary Eleanor could stand it no longer. She fled from their London home, where she had been held as a virtual prisoner, and sued for divorce, citing her husband's repeated adultery. Stoney Bowes now faced bankruptcy if he lost the income he had been extorting from Gibside. He resorted to desperate measures.

On the afternoon of 10 November 1786, Mary Eleanor was kidnapped from her coach in Oxford Street by a band of Stoney Bowes's accomplices. After a wretched 33-hour journey, they reached Streatlam, where Stoney Bowes demanded that she drop the divorce suit, while he literally held a gun to her head. She refused. 'By God, you are an aston-ishing woman' was all he could say. By now Mary Eleanor's friends were in hot pursuit, and Stoney Bowes was forced to flee on horseback to Newcas-tle and then on to the open moor, still holding her at gunpoint. Finally, he was arrested after a scuffle at Neasham, and brought back to London to face trial. Ever resourceful, he feigned injury in an attempt to ingratiate himself with the court: he appeared 'dressed in a drab-coloured great coat, a red silk handkerchief about his head; he was supported by two men, yet nearly bent double with weakness, in consequence of his wounds'. He even commissioned scurrilous caricatures from the famous satirist James Gillray, who depicted Mary Eleanor as 'Lady Ter-magant Flaybum'. Despite this, he was convicted and imprisoned, but never gave up hope of regaining the estates that he still believed were rightfully his.

(Right) John, 10th Earl of Strathmore (1769–1820); after Mather Brown (collection HM Queen Elizabeth II)

Two years later, Mary Eleanor was finally granted a divorce. For the last decade of her life, she lived quietly in Purbrook Park in Hampshire, devoting herself to the care of her children and of her numerous small dogs.

JOHN, 10TH EARL OF STRATHMORE (1769–1820)

The 10th Earl had a grim childhood. He was neglected by his mother, who preferred his sisters, and bullied by his guardian, Thomas Lyon. After Cambridge, he served as a captain in the 64th Foot, but abandoned a military career in 1790 when he came of age and inherited his father's Glamis estates in Scotland. The 10th Earl restored family harmony: he was devoted to all his brothers and sisters by his

Mary Milner (d. 1860), who was the 10th Earl's mistress for many years and finally married him on the day before his death (Bowes Museum)

mother's two marriages and was reconciled with her. He also decided to buy out her life-interest in Gibside and Streatlam and settle in Co. Durham.

At Christmas 1790 the 10th Earl was invited to a performance of Nicholas Rowe's tragedy, *The Fair Penitent*, in the marble hall of Seaton Delaval, the towering Baroque mansion built by Vanbrugh near the Northumbrian coast. His eye was caught by Lord Delaval's beautiful daughter Sarah, who played Calista, the mistress of the original 'haughty, gallant, gay Lothario'. Her performance was praised by the *Newcastle Chronicle*: 'The most perfect judgment, taste and elegance characterised this amiable and accomplished female who is the darling of her family and deservedly the adoration of all this part of the world.' The festivities went on till eight the

next morning, and by then the Earl was 'desperately smitten'.

Sarah Delaval was called 'the wildest of her race', and the Delavals were a notoriously wild family. She is said to have danced naked at a regimental ball. In 1779, at the age of sixteen, she had been married off to the 2nd Earl of Tyrconnel, an easygoing friend of her father, who in 1787 bought Claremont in Surrey – ostensibly for the couple, but really so that she could be near her royal lover, Frederick, Duke of York, at Oatlands. In 1792 the 10th Earl bought Claremont Lodge to be near her for similar reasons. Sarah was also a frequent visitor to Gibside, from where she wrote in 1798: 'I continue to keep very good hours and take proper riding and walking exercise, though the former is only about the place, for the roads are awful'. Like the 9th Earl, she had contracted TB, and despite such exercise and doses of digitalis, she died at Gibside in October 1800, aged only 37. The 10th Earl, who had lost his mother only six months before, was grief-stricken. According to Augustus Hare:

He gave her a funeral which almost ruined the estate. Her face was painted like the most brilliant life. He dressed her head himself and then, having decked her out in all her jewels, and covered her with Brussels lace from head to foot, he sent her up to London, causing her to lie in state at every town upon the road, and finally to be buried in Westminster Abbey!

The 10th Earl set aside his private grief to revitalise Gibside after years of neglect. He seems to have begun remodelling the house in 1803; the date 1805 over the rebuilt Jacobean porch on the south front may mark the moment he returned to live in the house, but work continued until 1813. Lord Delaval had recommended a local architect, Alexander Gilkie, who retained the Jacobean bay windows with their deep mullions, but replaced the top storey with a battlemented parapet, perhaps to give the house a greater air of antiquity. The 10th Earl also completed his grandfather's chapel, abandoning Paine's proposal for elaborate coffering on the interior of the dome, but commissioning a huge three-decker pulpit, which, in accordance with early nineteenth-century liturgy, gives greater prominence to the preacher than to the altar.

In 1809 the 10th Earl met Mary Milner, a house-maid at Wemmergill Hall, his shooting box in Yorkshire. She became his mistress and gave birth to a son, John, in 1811. According to the midwife, he 'seemed very pleased it was a boy'. He acknowledged the child as his own, and altered his will to leave him all his English estates. Mary Milner and Lord Strathmore lived together at Wemmergill and Streatlam, but her position was difficult. She would sit at the head of the table when they dined alone, but never if there was company, and she never visited Gibside during his life. None the less, when he received an additional English peerage in 1815, he took the title of Baron Bowes of Streatlam and Lunedale, where he had met Mary, and in 1820 he decided to marry her. By then, he was seriously ill and had to be carried into the church in a sedan chair. But he declared it to be one of the happiest moments of his life. It was also one of the last, for he died the following day. His body was carried north for burial in Gibside chapel, accompanied by his wife-for-a-day, and their nine-year-old son.

JOHN BOWES (1811–85)

Who was now to be the 11th Earl of Strathmore? John Bowes claimed that under Scottish law his parents' marriage retrospectively legitimised him and that the Scottish earldom was therefore rightfully his. But the 10th Earl's younger brother Thomas made a rival claim, which was upheld by the courts, who also awarded him the family's ancestral Scottish estates at Glamis. Gibside and Streatlam, however, passed to plain John Bowes, as he remained. While he was growing up, they were managed by his mother, who lived quietly at Gibside until her death in 1860. In 1831 she married her son's former tutor, William Hutt, who went on to have a distinguished parliamentary career. As Augustus Hare explained, she calmly accepted the social stigma that still clung to her position:

Lady Strathmore always behaved well. As soon as she was a widow, she said to all the people whom she had known as her husband's relations and friends that, if they liked to keep up her acquaintance, she should be very grateful to them, and always glad to see them when they came to her, but that she should never enter

John Bowes (1811–85), about 1830; by Joseph N. Negelen (Bowes Museum)

any house on a visit again, and she never did. ... She was a stately woman, still beautiful, and she had educated herself since her youth, but, from her quiet life (full of unostentatious charity) she had become very eccentric.

John Bowes doted on his mother and was a conscientious landlord of Gibside and Streatlam, from whose stud he sent out a succession of Derby winners, trained by John Scott, 'the Wizard of the North'. These included in 1853 the legendary 'West Australian', which also won the 1,000 Guineas and the St Leger – the first winner of the Triple Crown. But he preferred to enjoy his considerable wealth among the artistic circles of Paris, where his illegitimacy was no social barrier. Like his father, he fell in love with an actress, Mlle Joséphine Benoîte Coffin-Chevalier, la Contessa di Montalbo, for whom he bought an entire theatre in Paris. After their marriage in 1852, they settled in the château of Louveciennes, and began creating a superb collection of Spanish and French Old Master paintings and decorative arts of all kinds. In 1869 they founded the Bowes Museum at the small market town of Barnard Castle, not far from Streatlam, to house the collection, bringing an astonishing splash of continental culture and Renaissance architecture to the bare moorlands of the Tees Valley.

LATER HISTORY

When John Bowes died at Streatlam in 1885 his body was brought by special train to be placed in the family crypt of Gibside chapel alongside his wife's coffin. Since they had no children, Gibside and the Bowes family heirlooms reverted to the Strathmores, with whom John Bowes had re-established good relations.

The Strathmores now owned four large houses, but concentrated their efforts on maintaining the ancestral seat at Glamis and the more convenient house at St Paul's Walden Bury. Gibside House was let and during the First World War was used by land girls, but by the 1920s it had been abandoned and the interiors removed. George Bowes's landscape garden declined more slowly; as a child, the late Queen Mother, daughter of the 14th Earl of Strathmore, made occasional visits from Streatlam for picnics in the park at Gibside. Streatlam was sold in 1922 and finally demolished with high explosives in 1959.

The architectural writer Christopher Hussey, writing about Gibside for *Country Life* in 1952, described the scene:

The statue of British Liberty surveys from its column a scene of tragic desolation. Thickets of scrub and brambles and willow herb alone mark the woodlands of one of the grandest idylls created in the eighteenth century.

Gibside House lost its roof and floors in the 1950s, and James Paine's Chapel might have gone the same way if the National Trust had not restored it in 1965. With the Long Walk and with covenants protecting other parts of the estate, it was given to the Trust by the executors of the 16th Earl of

Strathmore in 1974. In 1993, the Trust acquired another 353 acres (143 ha) of the park, with the aid of a National Heritage Memorial Fund grant. This comprised the historic core of the Gibside estate, including the ruins of Gibside House (consolidation began in 2002), the Column to Liberty (repaired in 1994) and the Orangery (consolidated 2004). With further help from the NHMF, the old home farm at Cut Thorn was bought in 1997; the enclosed park fields, together with the riverside meadows of Warren Haugh and Lady Haugh, followed in 1998.

In 2004, with the support of the Heritage Lottery Fund, the National Trust acquired the former Stables and began an extensive scheme of restoration, with the conversion of parts of the building to accommodate working and study groups. Repairs to the Orangery will stabilise the building and allow the replanting of some of the interior flower-beds. An extensive programme of thinning the woods and conifer plantations throughout the estate is being undertaken in partnership with the Forestry Commission. This will eventually restore the woodlands to their historic layout and help realise once more George Bowes's grand design for the landscape of Gibside.

'Gibside Mr Chips' being led out from the Gibside Stud, just before restoration work commenced on the Stables in 2004